i hate that i love u.

Miley Rae Hurley

Sunshine & Moonbeams
Publishing

Copyright 2024 Miley Rae Hurley

Sunshine & Moonbeams Publishing

All rights reserved.

The characters and events portrayed in this book are real.

Any similarity to real persons, living or dead,

is not coincidental and was intended by the author.

No part of this book may be reproduced,

or stored in a retrieval system,

or transmitted in any form or by any means, electronic,

mechanical, photocopying,

recording, or otherwise, without express written

permission of the publisher.

Manuscript is printed in Cambria, 10 pt

For information about Sunshine & Moonbeams Publishing

and/or Miley Rae Hurley, please visit

https://mileyhurley10248.wixsite.com/sunshinemoonbeamseve

Cover design by Miley Rae Hurley

Manufactured in the United States of America

ISBN 979-8-9912518-0-8 (pbk)

*This book is for
anybody who has been
pushed to the side
and made to feel
like a second choice
in their own story.*

i hate that i love u.

Miley Rae Hurley

Preface

The words that you are about to read within the following pages are the truth. They are not made-up fiction to please book-lovers like you and me. They are painfully true statements, each one of them, that ring true throughout my heart. I wish I could tell you that I was making it all up, but I'm not. For the next couple hundred pages or so, you will be reading every painstakingly upsetting, unguarded thought and feeling that I have had about a specific incident in my life. As you read, you should be able to piece together what that event is. (Kind of like a little scavenger hunt, huh?)

To the people that this book *is* about, if you happen to be reading this, I don't say names; I don't give significant details about your appearance; and I certainly don't expose you in any way, shape, or form. I wouldn't do that. While it is technically allowed in writing (if it's true, which this is), it's pretty wrong to do so. So, I won't. What I *will* do, though, is I will make sure you realize how deep of a gash you cut through me.

This is usually the part where the character in the book that has been hurt says something like, "I hope karma comes for you" or "I hope you feel the kind of pain that I felt," but I'm not going to say that here. No matter how hurt I am by what the both of you did to me, I would *never*, *EVER* wish that kind of heartbreak upon someone. Nobody deserves to be treated like that.

I hope all of the pain you caused me was worth the trouble for you both.

*If you would like to better understand
this book and the emotions
that have been poured into it,
I suggest listening to the
song, "the grudge" by Olivia Rodrigo.*

Anyways, enjoy.

Part 1

A Graveyard For A Broken Heart.

There is a moment
in your life
when you finally realize
what lays in front of you.

When you take off
the blindfold and you see
the destruction
unfolding before you.

That moment sucks, and for those
of you who haven't lived
through it yet, you're going to.
That is, unless you live
this perfect life
with a perfect family,

perfect grades,

and perfect friends.

Friends seem to be
the trouble for me.

I can latch onto them,
holding on until my tiny
fingers ache with pain.

Problem is, I just
can't seem to keep them.

The pain in my fingers
eventually becomes too much,
and I have to let go.

Friends always leave
my life, coming and
going like the seasons
on the earth.

Fluttering to the ground
like dead leaves.

It's not because
I'm a bad person.

I'm not.

Or, not since the
last time I checked…

People just…

…go their separate ways.

Sometimes they don't come back.

Other times, though,
they do.

Even when they really shouldn't.

But how are you
supposed to know whether or
not you should come back?

How should
anyone know?

You can't know.

Coming back is a choice.

It's not fate.

You decide what you want to
happen, and then you act on it.

Does everything turn
out like you wanted?

Hopefully.

That's kind of
the kicker
in life though,
isn't it?

You can run
through scenario
after scenario
in your head
about what you
want to happen.

But, statistically speaking,
that scenario is
likely to never
happen.

Perhaps it
never even had the
possibility
of existing
in the first place.

When I first met
my best friend, I thought
I had found the kind of
love that everyone talks about
in books and movies.

The kind of love
that goes down
in history, like
Antony and Cleopatra,
or Marie and
Pierre Curie.

Except...
best friends...

Maybe not that
extreme, but...

A love that was supposed
to last.

You see, the ironic
thing is that both
of the aforementioned
legends have faults.

Typos in the script.

They both end.

Did I do that
on purpose?

No.
I didn't.

These were the first
two that I thought of.

Both ending
in tragedy.

Antony and Cleopatra.

They were both
madly in love.

And it was meant
to stay that way, right?

Right...?

Wrong.

They die.
Both of them.

They kill themselves
because neither of them could
obtain what they wanted.

A girl and a kingdom.

Marie and Pierre
Curie.

They were best friends.
Partners in their field.

They worked
side-by-side each day.

Until one day,
Pierre died.

His skull was crushed
in a mere freak-accident
in the street.

And Marie?

She died holding on
to the one thing she loved.

You think you
can love someone
unconditionally.

You think you
can love them
and that there is
absolutely nothing
they can do that can
mar your friendship.

That is…

Until they cause
the one unthinkable,
inconceivable, irreversible
damage that you so falsely
believed they would never inflict.

And if you're like me, you're
too blind to see it.

Knowing something
is going to hurt you
before it actually does
is a really important
skill to have in life.

But how are you
supposed to see
one single thorn
on an otherwise
perfect rose?

How could you
possibly be worried
about something that you are
so sure isn't meant to happen?

You can't argue
with the universe
when it decides that you
and another person
aren't meant to be.

Making friends has
always been
relatively difficult
for me.

I should say,
it's more of the "warming up"
to them idea that
I can't grasp.

So, when she walked
up to me with her
perfect hair and her
perfect smile,
her kind words and
her friendliness,
of course I would trust her.

How can you not
love an angel when
you don't see the
devil behind its eyes?

We were in our
physical education
class when I first met her.

Met her officially,
I mean.

I had known about
her because of my dad.

He had informed
me that she and I
were cousins.

I was excited, of course.

I knew it would be…
~~painful.~~
~~damaging.~~
~~heartbreaking.~~
amazing.

I hear so many people
who have gone
through heartbreak,
whether it be the death of a
loved one, or
a breakup, get asked
the question,
"If you could go
back in time
and do it all again,
would you?"

I never knew what
I would say to someone if they
were to ask me this.

I've never thought
about it, and,
to be honest,

I never thought
I would have to.

The day we met,
I remember
going home to my
mom and telling her
all about what had
happened to me that day.

I was thrilled —
my little face
enlightened with
joy, happiness, and hope.

I was brimming
with thoughts of
all of the new experiences
I would have with
my new friend.

Experiences that I
should look back on
and smile at,
but I don't.

Most people love
having memories.

They should, right?

They're a great
thing to have.

But making new
memories scares me.

The reason?

A very sad amount
of memories that I have made
with friends have only
left me in tears down the road.

Frankly, I don't appreciate
being left in such a state.

Have you ever
cried so hard over
someone that your
heart *literally* hurts?

Have the tears
pouring out of
yours eyes ever
cut red, burning lines down your
face like tiny, vicious claws?

Have your lungs
burned so hard
that every breath feels like
swallowing blue fire?

Have you ever
had a knife plunged
through your back...
...by your best friend?

There is a word
that I want to talk about.

Betrayal.

This word...
it hits a particular
nerve in my heart that just
rubs me the wrong way.

It stings me, like
stepping on a bee.

But there is no bee.

There is no stinger.

Only broken fragments, shards,
pieces of a broken heart,
left to rot.

They say that time
heals all wounds.

I don't know
who the heck was high when
they wrote that,
because *NEWSFLASH!*
it doesn't.

Sure, you learn
to live with certain
types of pain, but the
pain leaves scars behind.

And scars don't heal.

No amount of time
can ever truly heal a scar.

Especially when the
cut is too deep.

You might say,
"Oh, well you haven't
given it enough time
to heal properly!"

No.
No.

NO.

Don't give me
that nonsense.

You don't have to
have a master's in
rocket science or be a doctor
to know that some cuts are
just too deep.

Why can't people
just accept that?

When she told
me that I needed to,
"get over it,"

I thought she was right.

I was convinced for
the longest time that I was the
one in the wrong for feeling
the way that I do.

I've given it some
thought, though, and
I'm not in the wrong.
She is.

How do you tell somebody that
they need to just-
Get. Over. It.

You can't.

By all means,
technically,
you *can*.

But just because
you *can*, doesn't mean
you *should*.

How do you
expect a person to simply
forget how they feel?

To toss aside their
feelings to, what, make
you feel better about
yourself and what *you* did?

Yeah, my bad.

I didn't mean to hurt
your feelings.

Here's some advice.

Take it from me when I tell you
that you need to start focusing
on yourself more.

No, not in a
selfish, egotistical way.

Definitely not that.

I mean in a way
to better yourself —
to make sure
you are doing okay.

See, I failed to do this.
For the *longest* time.

Big mistake.

If you're anything
like me, you get attached to
people extremely easily.

Getting attached to
someone like I do can be…

…well…

Detrimental.

To your health.
To your mind.
And to your heart.

The grief of their
presence, or lack
thereof, claws at you,
eating away at your insides until
they are nothing more than
tattered scraps.

You can hold on
to one person,
like a child
holding onto a balloon.

When they fly
away, you look
for them frantically,
searching that sea of
blue, that field of
fluffy clouds, until you
lose yourself trying to salvage
that bright color of
the rubber and latex that
you once held so close.

Once you get it back,
though, you notice
that it's damaged.
And in case you
didn't know…
…damaged balloons pop.

On the subject
of balloons, they
scare me sometimes.

Not in general, just when
they get loose and
fly away.

Powerlines act
like tripwire,
set off at the slightest
of movement,
entangling anything
that crosses its path
within its live wires.

A lost balloon is
sensitive to every
risk of corruption.
And if you haven't
already realized,
this wasn't about balloons.

I could keep talking about
balloons for a while.

But I won't.

Not for several
more pages, anyways.
(Don't worry, I'll
make it interesting
when we get there.)

I want to talk about
something brand new, now.

Not something I
made up or anything.

A new topic.

Weasels.

By usual definition, a weasel is a
small, carnivorous mammal.

But most already know that.

What people don't always
know is that there is an
alternative definition.

To quote *Google*, a weasel can also be
"a deceitful or treacherous person."

Sounds about right.

Do you know any?
If you do, I'm sorry.

But if you're saying you don't,
you probably do and have
fallen into their trap.

The weasels *I* know?

Not the mousy little
rodents that walk
on four legs and squeak.

They walk on two
legs, and they *blab*.
Not squeaking.

Blabbing.

In the off chance
that you're wondering
what that is, *blabbing* is when a
person feels the need to let everyone
know how they feel or
what they are doing.

Those are the weasels
that *I* know.

If you've never
known or
been aware of
what this kind of
weasel looks or
acts like, I'll
tell you from
my experience.

They tend to be someone close to
you, but not always.

The ones I know
like to be close to you,
but not *too* close.

They approach from
the side, sneaking
up on you like
a predator, just to
make you...
...*uncomfortable*?

Crazy, right?

From my experience, there are three goals
that these kinds of people have.

1. Make you jealous.
2. Embarrass you.
3. Make you miserable.

Why, exactly?

I have literally no idea.

Let's be honest here.
How sad is it for a person
to make *their* entire goal for
the day be in making *you* feel awful?

Really, really sad.

It's so sad that you almost,
almost feel some ounce
of pity for them.

But you don't.

Or you shouldn't,
anyways.

Sometimes, they'll
make so much of an
effort to annoy you
or bother you that you almost
crack up with laughter.

I know I have.

Of course, not to their faces.

That would be rude.

God forbid I be
rude, though, right?

Another thing about
them is that literally no
one ever has any idea
what they are doing.

It's as if everyone is so unaware of
their behavior that it almost feels
like you're imagining it.

You know you're not.

But they still make
you feel like you're…
…dramatic?
…mean?
…crazy?

Yeah.

It's one thing to think
something about yourself.

But to hear it
from another person
as well…?

That stings. A lot.

To clarify, I didn't
think that I was being
mean or dramatic.

But I did feel
like I was crazy.

This was completely
irrational, though,
because I knew I was absolutely
correct for being upset about
what she did.

Some people will
try to make
themselves look
better in certain
scenarios.

If they look
like the *bad guy*,
they'll try to twist
things, bending and molding the
truth in their angry, hard fists
until nobody even knows
what the truth is
anymore.

Unless you're the one
who is reminded
every day of the truth,
and you know it
in your soul.
Even when it's muddled
to everyone else.

There are several
methods, or tactics, that
people can use to hide the truth.

One of these is
straight-up lying.

That's pretty basic,
though, that's not
to say that it works any
less efficient.

The other way is
constantly telling you
that you're remembering
it wrong.

Especially if you
have told them
previously that you
have a bad memory.

No, this doesn't
mean that everybody
who says this is trying to
cover something up.

To be more specific,
they will take your
weakness and turn
it into their strength,
manipulating your brain
to make you think
that you are just really
good at forgetting.

Do you honestly think
that I have *that* bad
of memory to the point where
I would forget the
things you've done?

I don't forget
my scars.

Trying to tell someone
that they are incorrectly
recalling the past when they
know that you hurt them is
called gaslighting.

More specifically when
they know you aren't
always the best with memory.

Don't believe me?
Look it up.

Friends aren't supposed
to do that to you.

I should've never heard
this phrase out of her mouth:
"Oh, well you have a bad memory,
so how would you know
that I did that?"

I know.

I don't have dementia,
thank you.

The concern is much
appreciated, though.

I mean, did she honestly think she
could fool me into thinking that I just forgot
everything about our friendship?

I remember when people hurt me.

I remember when they take their
thorny words and rake them
across my beating heart.

I remember every memory,
good or bad.

I should've known
it would end terribly.

Of course, it was nearly impossible to have
known, but looking back now, I see things
that I didn't before.

For one thing, she had the iciest blue
eyes I have *ever* seen.

In person, anyway.

They were sparkly,
shiny, and *cold*.

Back then, they reminded
me of a constellation, bright and beautiful.

Now they remind me
of icicles.

Don't get me wrong,
icicles *are*
beautiful.

I always loved
knocking them off
of the gutters of
my childhood home,
and it was always so
pretty when they
would shatter on the
concrete below, scattering
around little shards of
ice like mini
kaleidoscopes.

But icicles hurt
when they break away from the
frozen, cold steel and pierce
that first layer of skin.

An icy bullet.

Beautiful things
often hide the most
evil secrets.

Do you ever notice
how the prettiest
girls in movies are often the
most cruel?

There is a reason for that.

They are capable
of using their
innocent looks
and their "harmless"
games to toy with people's
minds, dragging them down
into their never ending
façade of shiftiness and control.

And no one ever knows.

Few will ever
realize in time that they
are slowly falling
deeper and deeper
into an inescapable
trap.

Getting out of
the trap
is like gasping
for air and
not getting any.

Reaching for a ledge when
there isn't one to hold on to.

Fighting for
a friendship when you
know that the person
you're fighting for
has already set you free
a long time ago.

The time I
first realized
how much she
truly meant to me
was when she left on a trip
to one of her favorite places.

Disney World.

She was so excited to go, and
I was excited for her.

But when she left,
I fell apart.

I was so distraught,
crushed that my
best friend had left me.

I had no idea what
was down the road.

I hugged her so
tightly before she left.

Not only was
the sadness of her departure
engulfing me, but
the fear of something
happening to her as well.

Anything could
happen to someone
if they stop paying attention for
even a second.

Car accident.
Robberies.
Natural disasters.
Illness.

All of which would
not affect her.

We've made it
pretty far, here.

At this point in time,
you are probably
wondering why or
how I lost my best friend.

Maybe. Unless you've figured
it out from my
previous statements,
in which case, good job. Or,
unless you're the
lost best friend.

If not, though,
I am about to tell you.

I hope you're comfortable
because you might
be here awhile.

I've already told the
first part of our story.

We met, we became close
with each other,
and she went on a trip.

However, what I
haven't told you
is that despite
how close we became,
we still fought often.

About. Anything.

We argued, as the
expression goes,
like a married couple.

I never knew best friends
fought so much.

If one of us did
the slightest thing to upset
the other by accident? Fight.

Said something
wrong? Fight.

Offended them in
some way
unintentionally? Fight.

I'll admit, I was half
of the reason we fought so much.

Close friendships like
what we had take a duel effort.

Both parties contributed.

One party lost the war.

We got much better
as time went on.

We fought less.

Bonded more.

Throughout the two
summers that we knew each
other, we tried to spend
as much time together
as our parents would allow.

We swam at her
grandma's house.
We baked cakes just
to eat them out of a cup. We'd
go out to her trampoline in the
backyard and gaze
at the stars, searching
for constellations.

I would kill for a
moment like that back.

One more day.

One.

More.

Night.

Of happiness. Joy. Love.

No more pain.
No more heartbreak.
No more anger.

I want the sleepovers back.
I want the coffee dates back.
I want *her* back.

My heart and
my brain tend to
agree on the same
things.

Except for this.

I know, deep down,
that she's gone, and
her coming back
will *never* be anything
remotely close to a good idea.

But my brain…
…it just won't
let her go. It can't.

It's like an infection,
spreading and
growing each time
you're exposed to the virus.

I'm sure you've been sick before,
and I'm sure if you have,
you have likely taken medication
to lessen the symptoms.

I wish there was
a medication to aid with grief.

Genuinely aid with it,
not just make you happy.

Not just a false happiness.

Would I take it?
I don't know.

Probably not.

I've never been good
at swallowing pills.

You know
what pills
remind me of?

The truth.

Having just one
small dose can irritate you
and make you
want to spit it back up.

But having too much…
…can kill you.

And as you lay there,
your body desperately
trying to rid
your system of
the toxins, you think,
"What could I have
done to save myself?"

Part 2

A Slow Fall Into Nothing.

Best friends are supposed
to be there for each other.

And we were.

For the most
part, anyways.

I always came to
her competitions,
and she always
came to my choir concerts.

I cheered her up when she
was sad, and she did
the same for me.

There was one
distinct time in my life,
though, when it didn't
work that way.

It was the day of the student
government elections in
our middle school.

I was running
for president.

My main competition
was against this guy who
I guess you could say
was pretty popular.

Other people had
already announced that they
would be voting for him.

Worried, I still ran.

Afterall, I'd have some
people in my corner...
...right?

Lunchtime.

Her and I are sitting at our
lunch table discussing how
nervous I am for
the results of the election.

I tell her that I'm
scared, even though
I already knew who
would win.

Out of nowhere, she
tells me that she is going
to sit elsewhere.

Not with me.

I was scared out
of my mind and she
just left me.

She had never,
ever sat somewhere
else before.

She told me it was
because she wasn't
feeling well, but she's felt sad
or ill at lunch before and she
has still *never* left me.

Why now?

Why on one of the biggest school
days for me did she have to leave?

Watching her walk
away felt like a knife
through my heart.

That afternoon, I cried
instead of eating.

Sitting by yourself
at lunch has got
to be one of
the *worst* feelings
a teenager can experience.

Especially when the
person you're meant
to sit with turns
their back on you.

Nobody asked
how I was doing
the rest of the day.

I was upset and
distraught and nobody cared.

At least, not until
the results of the
election were read.

He had won by a landslide.

I didn't even come
in second place.

Although I wasn't entirely
surprised, it still stung.

I just wanted to
leave and go home.

But she still asked me
how I was doing.

"Are you okay?"
"I'm sorry he won."
"I voted for you."

I didn't want her
pity. Not then, and not now.

Now, don't take
what I said the wrong way.

I have sat somewhere
else during lunch as well.

Did I leave her on an
emotional day?

No.

Was it still wrong?

Yeah, it was.

I am not at all trying to say that
I was some perfect friend.

I was far from it, but that doesn't
justify any wrongdoings.

What did I do, exactly?

Well, I'll tell you.

The truth.

Not some
watered-down
version of the
truth.

Not a version
that will falsely
make one of us look bad.

Not even a version
that you tell to people to hide your
own guilt and shame.

The *real* truth.

We had just
began our highschool
careers as freshmen.

We were every bit
as scared and nervous
as the next girl, desperately hoping
that we didn't get separated
from each other
at lunch with there
being two different
hours for it.

Lunch A and Lunch B.

We both made it into
Lunch B, and we were relieved.

We decided to sit
with each other
every day.

Same time.
Same routine.
Same place.

We, for the most
part, sat by ourselves.

There were several empty seats between
us and the other people at the table.

It was nice.

Was.

But we still had a
tendency to fight.

When we fought,
lunch would be awkward
and just downright uncomfortable.

We wouldn't talk.
We'd sit on our phones.

Silence.

The one time of
day that we got to freely
socialize and
I wasn't doing it.

Couldn't.

I had a boyfriend
at the time. He said he
would've loved it if I
sat by him at lunch.

With him knowing
what I just told you,
him and his friends said I
was welcome to join them.

I considered my options,
weighing them carefully.

I decided to move.

I felt guilty, yeah,
but to be entirely
honest, I'm glad I moved.

Or, I *was*.

I knew it would
hurt. Hurt her, I mean.

It hurt me, too.

But I had no idea
that the one decision
I made that day would
cost me my best friend.

She told me
it was *my* fault.

When I moved, she
went to sit with someone who I
used to be friends with.

But we had a falling out.

And I didn't like her.

My best friend knew
this, and she still
sat with her.

They barely knew each other, and there
were over a hundred other people in
that room she could've sat with instead.

She blamed it on me.

It's *my* fault that
you chose the one
person that I can't
be around to get
close with??

Umm, no.

That was your choice. *You*
decided that, not me.

Did I know
she would do
something like that?

Absolutely not.

I never would've
even begun to imagine
she'd do anything
close to that.

If I would have
known she would
do what she did, I never would've
sat somewhere else.

I keep telling myself,
"You should've just stayed!"
"Why did you do that?"
"Why did you leave?

Why did *she* leave?

I didn't leave because I didn't
want to sit by her.

I didn't leave
because I would
rather sit by him.

I left because of the
constant fighting.

Pretty much
every fight that
we had leading up
to my leaving the
lunch table was due
in part to her being
upset with me over things that
you wouldn't generally
consider as being
triggering to most people.

In every apology,
she'd say that it was
because she was stressed
out from starting school.

Not a good excuse.

I was, too, and you
didn't see me getting
upset over every
little mistake.

You can't blame
that stress. Not
when every other
freshman was experiencing
the same thing.

And you certainly
don't take your
stress out, over anything,
on any*one*.

Especially when that
person is just
trying to be there for you.

Now, yes, I have
definitely done this before.

I'm sure everyone
has, whether you
mean to or not.

It doesn't make
you a bad person.

It's okay.

People make mistakes.

It's what you do
to change the
bad habit that counts.

Come to find out,
some things aren't
bad habits at all.

They're who we are.

Whether or not
you want it, you may
not even have a choice.

That's kind of
how it felt,
being friends
with her.

It was like she was always
stressed out in
some way for
whatever reason.

It didn't matter
when, how, or why.

It felt like all
I ever did was
get in the way
of the stress, or at some
times, even make it worse.

It just never
seemed to end.

When school began,
I completely
understood the
stress she was under.

Who wouldn't be
stressed out by
having to adjust to
an entirely new environment?

The stress didn't
bother me, but
using it as an excuse
for getting mad at me did.

Nobody deserves
that.

She didn't when
I did it to her, so why would
it be any different for me?

I have to stop
myself for just
a moment.

I need to clear the air.

The whole point
of everything
that I have told
you about this friend is not
to make her look like
a terrible person.

I definitely don't
want that.

What I *do* want
is for the truth to be heard.

Whether or not you
know who she is.

I've been
thinking, in the last
few days before I
ended things
with her, she told
me something.

Several times, actually.

"Everybody who
I've talked to
about it has thought
the same thing."

I disagree.

You see, I'm sure
some do, but I do
believe that you're
forgetting to tell
my side of the story.

That's the real
purpose of this book.

To get the truth,
the one that has
been pushed under
the rug, out.

Sometimes when we
recall events
that have happened between us
and another person,
we tend to leave
the other view out of it.

It's not necessarily
our fault. We can be totally
unaware that we are
even doing it.

But some do know.

Some people like to leave the
other view out on purpose.

This can be for many
different reasons. To name a few:

1. To play the victim.
2. To get support from others.
3. To make *you* look bad.

Maybe it's all
three at once?

That's a bad combo.

When somebody
leaves another person's
side of the story out in
their retelling, it can
twist things entirely.

Am I a bad person?

I don't know,
you tell me.

After reading this
book, I'd like
for you to think
for a minute and
decide what *you* think.

I had one goal
in mind when
retelling this story,
and that is to make
sure I tell both sides of
the story as fair as possible.
If something makes
someone look bad,
either her or I, it's not
intentional, it's simply the truth.

Now that that's
out, I can continue
with the story.

Where was I?
Oh right. She went to sit
with my...enemy?

No, that's not the word I want, but
I can't think of anything else, so
we'll go with that.

Let's think back.
The first day of school,
for me, was when everybody
was figuring out who was
in their classes.

There was never
a problem until
later in the day.

Her (my best friend)
and I had made it
to one of our last
classes of the day.

Since it was the
first day for everyone,
the teacher had not
yet assigned us
with a seating arrangement.
We were allowed
to sit wherever we wanted.

This freedom also
came with one small fault.

Not knowing
where to sit.

Or, rather, knowing
exactly where.

We had sat
down at a table,
and we were
thrilled that
we were able to
sit next to
each other.

However, there
was one *tiny* problem.

My enemy(?) was making her
way over to our table.

She just plopped
her stuff down and asked if
she could sit with us.

What were we
supposed to do, say no??

Obviously not.

Of course, I certainly
was *not* thrilled.

But there was nothing,
absolutely *nothing* that I could've
done to fix the way I was feeling.

I just had to suck
it up and deal.

I didn't speak
to her. Her and
my best friend barely
even knew each other
and they were talking like they'd
known each other for years.

I felt left out.
Like a ghost. Invisible.

Every day, I dreaded that
single class.

You know, I had
never felt physically
sick because of
a person before, until...

Them.

I watched them laugh
and smile together while
I sat there, nonexistent,
quiet, watching half
of my heart get torn
from my shredded chest.

That can't be...
They aren't
that close...
...right?

It felt like my
heart was being
doused with lighter
fluid and *they* were
striking the match.

My stomach was
churning and twisting itself into
an indiscernible ball of fear.

My brain was burning
with the inescapable
thoughts that I didn't even
want to consider.

I should've seen the signs.

I should've read
their moves.

But I was blind.

Sometimes, in chess,
when an opponent
makes a move that
is detrimental to
the game, it can
freak players out.

When you panic,
you fail to read
crucial moves and
signs that could
cost you the game.

Now, I've never played
chess, but I have seen people play,
and I've also seen
their poker face fall
apart under the pressure of a
sudden advantage gain from
the opponent.

It's frightening.

The reason why
it's so scary?
(Hint: It probably
isn't what you think.)

It's subtle.

The faint tilt of
the eyebrows.

Their mouth falling
from a straight line
into the tiniest frown.

The slightest adjustment of their
eyes, their gaze softening
into that quiet realization.

That heavy exhale of pent-up breath
that they've held in
to keep themself composed.

What's also scary is when
it happens to you.

It feels like everything in
the world stops.

Stops breathing.
Stops moving.
Stops *living*.

Realizing that you
now have the
lower hand of
a situation is
an awful feeling.

Especially when you
didn't have a say in it.

You're now the
butt of the joke.

My best friend
would ask me what was
wrong in that class.

I'd tell her it
was nothing.

She'd ask me later,
then, too.

When I would
finally tell her
what was really bothering me,
I'd be completely
honest. She would then
tend to get upset with me for not
wanting to work
with *that girl.*

It just got worse
as time went on.

There was a
particular day
that I can think
of where it got really bad.

We were in that
class and the teacher
had asked us to work
on a poster with
our groups, and she still
hadn't changed the seats.

I felt sick to
my stomach. I
did *not* want to work
with my enemy (that is
still not the right word,
but I'm at a loss for
words, so just hang
in there).

Here comes the misery.

The teacher instructed us on what to
do, and we got to work.

They did.

Not me.

I'm not proud of it, but I sat there
and talked to absolutely no one.

I didn't help with
the poster.

Or, at least, I wasn't
going to until my
"best friend" turned
to me and said,

"Are you going to help us
with this or not?"

I responded in a whisper with,
"I don't want to work with *her*."

Something changed in her.

Morphed.

Like a snake
shedding its skin.

She had *snapped*.

"You're *supposed* to
be working on this
with us as a group. You
won't get credit if you just
sit there and do nothing."

I was shocked. Taken aback.
Absolutely *appalled*.

She had *never*
raised her voice
at me before.

Never.

I felt as if the whole
class had heard what she said.

I immediately
held my tongue.

I didn't know
what to do, how to act, or
even what to say.

The embarrassment
had flooded me
in a tidal wave
of shame, guilt,
and bittersweet regret.

Regret.

The words painfully
rake across my chest, even now.

I should have
seen it sooner.

I should have
protected myself.

I had opened
up like a flower
to the first person willing
to show me what love
and admiration looks
like in friends.

I had unknowingly
placed my heart
in the hands of a monster.

I should have given
up sooner.

Why didn't I just *let her go?*

I loved her so, *so* much.

Loved.

I would've fought for her.

I would've taken
a bullet for her.

A *hundred* bullets.

Just. For. *Her.*

Not anymore, though.

That's what I
tell myself,
anyways.

I know full-well
that I would
still take those bullets
for her.

Every last one of them.

No matter how
much pain she has
caused me, no matter
how many times I have
cried because of her,
nothing, *nothing* can
ever make me stop loving her.

And I
hate that.

There is a
special kind of
pain that you
experience when
you love or want
something that you know you
can't ever have.

My God, does it *hurt*.

It is single-handedly
the most painful
thing I have ever experienced.

And it doesn't leave.

The worst part
is knowing that that
person may never know
how much you really
love them.

This type of pain hurts
even more when you can't stop
having thoughts about it.

So.
Many.
Thoughts.

Like,
"We will never
do ____ again."

Or,
"We will never
have a sleepover again."

Or the worst one,
"I'll never hug her again."

Cause I won't.
Ever again.

What hurts me
the most is the
truth that I just
don't want to face yet.

But I know I have to.

I know that even
if she ever came
to me to apologize
or ask to be friends
again, I have to say no.

We *can't.*

No matter how
badly I miss everything
we built together, I have to watch
our city continue
falling apart, until
the debris is gone.

Nothing but
ash and *dust.*

That is what is left of
our friendship.

Broken fragments
of memories, times
we lost to the cruel hand of time
and the cold steel of a knife
stuck in your back.

Times that I look back
on and feel hurt.
Angry.

Torn.

The line between
love and hate is
oh-so thin.

I remember crying
one time because
of her.

I've cried many
more times, of course,
but this one in
particular sticks out to me.

I was crying in my
bathroom, leaning against
the wall for support,
feeling like my heart
was being ripped
out of my chest.

The love that had
bloomed for her going
right along with it.

I could hardly breathe.

Wow, I've went
on such a rant about
everything, you still don't
know the rest of the story.

Sorry about that.

After she practically
yelled at me, I
helped with the project.

But I wasn't letting
what she said go.

I can't really
remember if we got
into an argument
about it later, but I'm
sure we did.

I was *mad.*

Did I let her
know I was mad?

Oh yeah.

I gave her the
most fuming, tortured look
that I could muster.

Like an injured animal.

It didn't take much
effort. It had
appeared before
I even knew it.

I don't usually give people
looks like that.

But, *that* was necessary.

One of the things
that makes me so
mad about that event
is that we weren't
even fighting
when it happened.

We were doing
just fine earlier in the day.

She would just
always get so
upset with me for
hating this one person.

I wasn't rude to her.

Sure, I didn't like her,
and I avoided her,
but I was never
rude about it.

The only thing
that I ask of them is to simply
stay away from me.

I don't care that
you're friends, okay?

I'm done trying to fight for things
to go back to normal.

If they ever were.

I just ask that you
leave me alone.

It is *not* that difficult to mind
your own business and keep your
distance unless absolutely necessary.

It's quite simple, actually.

I've been doing
it easily for months.

The problem is them.

No, I'm not trying to talk
bad about them.

I'm telling the truth.

Every time I talk
to someone, whether
they know them
or not, those two are
always finding some
reason to speak to them
when we are in the middle
of a conversation.

They go out of their
way to do it, too.

They also talk about things they
already know about
each other, as well.

Right in front of me.

Like, I know you
both already know
about the gifts you've
gotten each other.

There's no need
to repeat them.

It's very obvious
that their talking about
these things isn't just for some
idle conversation.

And it's something
that nobody seems to notice.

That doesn't really
bother me, though.

It's just kind of annoying.

What's even more annoying is seeing the
person you love *so much* grow close
with another person. If not *closer.*

No, not annoying.

Frightening.

Knowing that you
have absolutely no
power to stop what
you are witnessing.

They have every
choice, and you have none.

I don't want to just talk
about the bad parts.

Or, not yet, anyways.

We had so many
good memories,
like all of the band
concerts I went to
for her, and the school
trips we attended
together.

Oh, but my personal
favorites were all
of the times we
would call and
play that horror
game she and I loved.

It never got boring.

The way we would always
tell the other one
to go first because
we'd be too scared.

(She was always the bravest
out of the two of us.)

The way we knew
the different levels by heart.

The way we'd shriek when
the bad guy got us.

Now she plays it
with her new friend.

Me?

Nope.

Not to say that
she isn't allowed
to play it with
other people.

Of course she is.

But you'd think
after how many
hours we played it,
and how many times we had
planned to play it, it would mean
a little something more than
just being a game.

You'd think it wouldn't be
that easy to just *move on.*

Was it?

Was it easy for you?

My question is,
"Do you have as
much fun playing it with her
like you did with me?"

I hope you have fun.

I hope you
laugh so hard it hurts
because you get so
scared about a little
monster on a screen.

You having fun
would mean at least
one of us is.

I haven't logged onto that game
since the last we played.

It hurts too much.

Another one of
my favorite memories
was when her and I made
this video of us dancing in
one of our local playgrounds.

We sent it to our friend, to
which she found it hilarious.

I still have the
video.

"But do you?"

I was in my green
hoodie that day.

Gosh, my hair looked *so* bad.

But she didn't mind it.

Later that
day, we had a
sleepover at
your house.

We had so much fun.

I'm pretty sure that was
one of the nights
where we made
some scrappy cake
out of her pantry,
slapped some icing
on only my portion
because she didn't like
icing, and eat it outside
under the stars in the dark.

We even swirled the
batter ourselves with
the extra chocolates
that she had.

Oh my gosh,
one night we had
cake and it
made me so sick.

I didn't go home, though.

That was how
comfortable
I was with her
and her family.

They always made
me feel so welcome.

It felt like a second
home for me.

So, you could only imagine
how it felt to have lost
that place.

We used to go to the public pool, too.

It took me forever to
get her to come with
me, but she caved eventually.

She had to admit,
it was *really* fun.

We would jump
into the pool so many times.

We'd do it until we got tired
and had to stop.

Tired?
Yes.

Bored?
Never.

There was also a time when we
made this poster of two
lobsters with our feet.

It was *hilarious.*

We painted the
bottoms of our feet
red with acrylic paint, and we
stamped on their features.

We used our hands
to form the claws.

Once we were
done, we got in my
bathtub and washed our
feet of the paint.

There is still a red
smear on the curtains.

One night recently, I was
crying about our friendship.

After it had failed.

I was looking through old pictures
and videos that we had of each other.

Specifically the one
of us dancing.

That broke me.

I went to bed shortly
after crying, and when I was sleeping, I had
a dream about us being friends with
each other again.

Kind of a sick joke for
my brain to play, huh?

This memory keeps
flashing through my
mind like a broken record.

It reminds me
of how fragile love and
compassion can be.

Her and I were
at the fair.

We loved the boat, so we went
on it *so* much.

I remember looking
into her eyes when the
ride was at the top, seeing
her smile with happiness.

I had told myself one
important thing.

This singular thing
would resonate
in my mind for years to come.

It always would.

"Remember this
moment; her happiness
and yours. Just in case
you happen to lose her."

So now, after
having had practically
zero contact with
her for months, these words *hurt*.

And so does the memory.

Knowing that I will *never*
be the cause of her pure
joy like that *ever* again.

How could I have known?

How could I
have seen what
I needed to look out for?

I didn't.

Thinking back, it actually makes me
realize that some things
don't have a long enough shelf-life.

Memories.

Friendships.

People.

And, for me…
Love.

I mentioned earlier how I can't
help but still love her.

Which is true.

I can't.

Another thing I can't do
is get the thought out of my head
that she doesn't feel the same.

Would *she* take those
bullets for me?

Would she?

I wouldn't blame
her if she refused to.

It's not like we're friends anymore.

Part 3

When It All Comes Crashing Down.

I'm just going to
start this out by saying that
this is going to be
a pretty long section,
so hang in there with me
for a little bit longer.

I promise, it gets much
more interesting from
here on out.

This is where I'll finally get
to tell you what happened.

What *really* happened.

Both sides of the story.

You ready?

I know you're not.

I tried not to look
too far into them
hanging out together
outside of school.

I'd tell myself that I was fine.

I wasn't hurting, and
everything was *okay*.

But it wasn't.

Every thought of
them having fun together,
every time I heard their
laughs, a new thorn was shoved into
my already-bleeding heart.

And, no, before
anyone tries to say
that it's jealousy, it's not.

Jealousy isn't being
in pain because
somebody you love
has picked someone
else over you.

It's not wishing you
could have just five more minutes
of friendship with
someone before this
new person came
and screwed everything up.

Do you want to
know what actual
jealousy is?

It's taking everything
a person loves from
them just to rub it
in their face like it's
some big accomplishment.

A lot of people
would probably argue
against me when I say that my
best friend was taken from me.

Which is fine.

But, here's the thing.

She *was* taken.

She doesn't even
realize what happened.

She allowed herself to
be stolen away from
her best friend by some other girl.

She just let her
waltz in and mess
everything up.

Why am I
accusing my
enemy of this?

It's not to make her look bad,
although frankly,
I couldn't care less if it did.

It's because she
has done it before.

Why do you think I call her
my enemy? Now
that I think about it,
it fits her perfectly.

Right after my enemy, this
one other person, and I got into
an argument, I pretty
much ended things with
the both of them.

Why?

They had slammed
my finger in a door.

Let me explain.

They were at my house, and I believe
I had left the room to go
tell my mom what we wanted
for dinner that night. When
I came back, my door
wouldn't open when I pushed on
it. So I pushed even harder.

When it still wouldn't
open, I made the
decision of trying to
pry the door open with my hands.

Bad decision, I know.

It cracked open for a second and
I had managed to slip
only one finger in
by accident (I meant
for my whole hand to
get through).

Next thing I knew,
there was a white
door crushing my pointer
finger on my right
hand. My *drawing* hand.

I'm an artist, so if I were to break
any part of my right hand,
I fear that I will never
be able to draw the same.
So this was serious.

I yelled for them
to open up, that my finger
was stuck in the door.

I was yelling to what felt
like an empty void.

Nobody budged.

The door remained
clamped down on my finger.

They eventually let up,
and my finger was free.

But it was bruised
and it hurt *so* badly.

I went into my parents
room and cried for at least
five minutes while I heard them in
there giggling and not worried
about me at *all.*

Then my mom came.

She had been in
the living room, and she came
to see what was happening.

I told her through
my tears, and she brought
me to the kitchen so she
could go back and talk to
the girls in private.

When she returned,
she told them to apologize to me.

They did, saying that they
never heard me yell.

But the thing is,
my mom even heard me.

From all the way
across the house.

Listen, there is
no possible way
that I can know for
certain whether or
not they heard me, but prior to
that, neither of them had
ever mentioned having
any sort of hearing
difficulty, so I don't know how
they didn't hear me yell.

Their "apologies"
didn't fix a thing.

I begged my mom
to make them leave (not in
front of them, of course),
to which she said no.

She said they were our
guests and we couldn't
just kick them out.

I understood, even though
I still wanted them gone.

So, for the next maybe
two hours or so, I pretended to be
okay with them being there.

I laughed. I smiled.

Down to the last second of them
walking out of my front door.

Once that door shut,
I didn't have to
pretend anymore.

I told my mom every
single detail.

And she messaged
both of their moms.

Naturally, both moms
sided with their child, saying
that they didn't mean it and that their
daughter apologized for the incident.

(What did you think
would happen?)

You are probably thinking, "Why are you
so mad about it if they apologized?"

Reasonable question.

Here are my
reasonings:

1. Their apology wasn't sincere.
2. They were disrespectful of my property.

I'll explain.

An apology isn't sincere
if a person has
to practically force
it out of you.

Neither are the
apologies saying,
"We are sorry! We
already said it. What
more do you want
us to say/do?"

Or something like that.

First of all,
it barely came
from you the first time.

Second of all, *I'm* not the one who
should be telling you what
to do to fix things.

You can't fix the disrespect
that they showed me.

Not with an apology.

The reason why
they were holding
the door shut was
because they were trying to keep
me out of my room.

Not to be funny, but to
hide something of mine.

Something I had
told them to put
away and not touch.

No, it wasn't valuable
or important, but I had asked
them not to touch it.

They did it anyway.

I had had a talk with one of
those friends previously
about respecting
my things and not touching them when
I ask them not to.

She clearly did
not get the message.

It should be a given,
though, right?

Whatever, the point
is that you don't lock someone
out of their own room
in their own house.

And they thought
it was okay?

I also have to add that while
I was crying in my
parent's bedroom
about what happened,
those two took pictures of
themselves on *my* phone.

What is the thought
process of what
they were doing??

I'd *love* to know.

We had all been best friends with
each other, for the most part,
for at least *eight years.*

Eight. Years.

All of it down the
drain in an instant.

The day after what
happened, I messaged
my (now) enemy and
asked her who it was
behind the door.

(Yes, that had been
a frequently argued subject.)

I believed it was her,
but she told me it
was our other friend.

I held firm to my
opinion, even
though I wasn't
in the room to see it.

At this point in time, I can't even
remember who I thought
was behind the door.

It doesn't matter,
though.

Either way,
they're both in
the wrong for trying
to keep me out
of my room.

I'll admit, I was in
the wrong for accusing
one person of something I didn't
even know the answer for myself.

I shouldn't have done that.

I should've apologized.

But I didn't.

And now it feels like war.

I have been fighting
a losing battle for *months.*

After the fight,
we were still going
to school, so we had
to see each other every day.

They sat in front
of me in one of our classes,
and every day, they would
put on a show right in
front of my eyes.

They would talk too
loud, even though they
were right next to each other, and they
would do everything together.

I knew it wasn't
real, though.

Previously to the
incident, my enemy
and I had spoken to each other
about the other friend.

It wasn't anything bad.

I had asked her why
they had woken me
up the way they had after one
of our sleepovers.

They had been running
around my room, jumping on my bed,
and yelling to try and wake me up.

They were also
hitting me with pillows.

I had been lying there,
awake, the whole time.

When I asked
her about it,
I told her I was
mad that they had
woken me up like that.

I told her it was rude and
annoying, which it was.

Her response?

She placed most
of the blame on
our other friend.

She told me that she
was just following along,
or that she tried to
get her to stop.

No. She didn't.

I was awake the entire time.

I heard everything
they said.

Not once did I hear anyone
hesitate or try to
calm the situation
down.

Real friends don't
pin the blame on
their friends.

Real friends don't lie
to their friends, either.

If they did, you wouldn't have
this story to read.

Thankfully, they don't.

So, why fake being best friends
with somebody?

That is something
I really *don't* understand.

I knew that they
weren't that close
with one another (yes,
I am talking about both
friendships — my enemy/our
other friend & my
enemy/my best friend).

In both friendships,
my enemy had admitted
to me that she was either
not that close with
the person (my enemy/our
other friend), or she
did not like the person (my
enemy/my best friend).

Yeah, I said it.

She didn't even *like*
my best friend
before she stole
her away from me.

That is how evil
she really is.

Nobody would ever believe me
because of how much of a face she
puts on when she's
around other people.

But she's not nice.

She'll never be the
person you think she is.

Never.

I told my best
friend about what
my enemy had told
me, that she didn't like her.

I didn't want to,
but I wanted to be
honest with her.

I wasn't trying
to ruin anything
between them, and
that is the absolute *truth*.

When I told her,
she didn't believe
me, so I asked her
if she wanted proof.

I showed it to her, and the
reaction left me utterly speechless.

I showed her the text messages
saying something along the lines of,
"...and that is why
(other friend's name)
and I don't like
(best friend's name)."

The screenshot even
included the contact
photo and contact
name, which I knew
was important.

What did my best
friend say to this?

"_(enemy's name)_
says that
isn't her."

....*what?*

I mean,
WHAT.

My heart had sunk
like an anchor.

My enemy was lying to her.

I hurried and typed
out a message
saying that I would
never lie to her,
especially about
something so important.

I told her I would never try
to ruin their friendship,
because I wouldn't, even
though it kills me.

I sent another picture.

The next picture
was of my enemy's
actual contact information so
my best friend could
check the phone number.

She showed it
to my enemy who says,
"That is NOT me.
I've never had a profile
picture like that."

That was the lamest
excuse I've ever
heard in my life.

Really??

No duh you haven't
seen the profile photo, it only
shows up in *my* phone.

I gotta be honest, that response had cracked me up.

I didn't think she was *that* bad at lying, but I guess I was wrong.

I told my best friend that reasoning, that there was no way for her to have seen her profile before.

A few minutes later, my best friend messages me this: "Ok nvm she said that she might have but idc."

Again…WHAT?

Jaw. Dropped.

What kind of
sneaky little weasel
does this girl think she is??

I was in disbelief.

She just changed
her response *so* quickly.

If someone does that,
how reliable do
you think they
really are?

I know she didn't just forget
what she said to me
about my best friend.

Also, it's in the past??

That excuse was
never valid before.

Not whenever *I'm*
in the wrong for something,
anyways.

Not whenever she
brought up what
happened at homecoming.

That will *never* be "in the past"
for her — *ever* — because she
never forgets when I
do something wrong.

I was never the
one she chose, and
I never would be, no matter how
many times she lied to my face
telling me I would be.

I will gladly explain
everything about
the homecoming
incident that I just
talked about, but first,
I want to mention something else.

Deserters.

Deserters are people who, according
to my personal experience,
give up on their friend(s)
simply because they are either
bored or have found something new.

Some*one* new.

There's another term
that means something
very similar, but it hits
the nail on the head more.

Friend poaching.

Ever heard of it?

I hadn't until about five minutes before writing this.

But hey, you learn something new every day, right?

Anyways, friend poaching is where two people befriend each other through your introduction and one starts putting more effort into their friendship than you do. This leads to both previous friendships with the two parties to be devalued and become less wanted.

Gosh, I hope that
made sense.

It probably didn't because I'm not
all that great at explaining things.

It's pretty much
what happened to me,
except one party
was no longer my
friend when it happened.

My enemy, essentially,
found her way to my
best friend and started
to show her more attention
than what I was showing her.

This does make me
sound bad, I know, but just...allow me
to explain what I mean.

I wasn't neglecting
our friendship or anything.

I just didn't think
I'd have to worry
about…poachers.

I texted her every
day, or I tried to,
and if I didn't, I
always felt bad for
not having done it.

I didn't think
someone would be able to weasel
their way in between
us so easily, but they did.

It caught me *so* off-guard.

Like, seriously.

Seeing them together felt
like getting slapped.

Like the air was
getting shoved out of
my lungs all at once.

Like my gut
was getting pricked
by hundreds of thousands
of tiny barbed wires that
leaked burning stomach
acid into my body.

Burning my skin.

My blood.

My heart.

Everything up in flames.

The only way
to put out the fire,
to patch up all of the tiny
holes, would be for them
to no longer be friends.

I couldn't ask that of my
best friend, obviously.

That wouldn't be right.

And even then, I'd
feel immensely
guilty about it.

I would never forgive myself.

Here's what I want
to know:
*Does my enemy
forgive herself?*

I don't know
how she could.

How she could even
live with herself after ripping
someone's heart out.

Forgiveness is a
difficult topic for some
people to talk about.

Most people say,
"You have to forgive
or else God won't forgive you."

Which I get for
certain people.

Not for me, though.

I don't work like that.

Like respect, forgiveness,
for me, is *earned*.

To me, just because you're
significantly older than
me, or just because
something is "in the past"
doesn't mean you have some right
to be forgiven or respected
by the people you did wrong.

If you don't give me
a reason to forgive
you or respect you, then I won't.

That's that.

Now, I'm not going
to be rude to this person,
but I definitely *will not* be
friendly with them.

Get mad at my opinion if you
don't agree, I don't care.

Your anger won't change my mind.

The two girls in this story,
my enemy and my (then)
best friend, seem to *expect* my forgiveness.

Lower your expectations.

It isn't happening.

Saying things like,
"Get over it."
"That was over a year
ago, let it go."
"She didn't do anything
to you for you to
be mad like this."
"She's already said sorry."

Band-Aids don't cover gaping wounds.

Fatal wounds.

Ones that cause
relentless bleeding
and leave unforgettable,
irreversible scarring.

Sorry doesn't instantly grant
you a forgiveness card.

It doesn't immediately
take away all the pain
that you have caused with
your carelessness.

Or your purpose.

Whatever it was that made
you who you are to me.

What are they,
you might be asking?

Monsters.

No, not the kind
with sharp teeth and ragged
breath and devilish eyes.

(Okay, actually, the
devilish eye-thing
is relevant in this case,
but they aren't obvious.)

They are the kind that lurk behind false
masks, revealing themselves
only when you're alone in the dark.

They won't ever
be caught because
nobody ever knows.

They run their
long nails along the wall, making
your brain itch with
the unrelenting irritation
of their presence that
never ceases to exist.

You know they're
always there, watching, waiting
for you to falter and mess up.

They want to see
you fail.

They want to
relish in your downfall
when it finally
happens, and you
know something
will because nobody
can be perfect
all of the time.

Every single time you enter a
room, no matter where it
is, you think,
"Where are they?"
"Are they here?"
"How do I avoid them?"
"What if I mess up?"
"What if they laugh?"
"How am I supposed to
react if they come
near me?"
"Why can't they
just leave me alone?"

It really is disgusting
that people, especially
past friends, can
make you feel so
scared for yourself
in any environment.

Even your own home.

That shouldn't
even be possible.

But it is.

That is how accustomed I've
grown to having to
look out for them.

To having to defend
myself against such a simple thing
as their *presence*.

I *hate* that they
wield that power to
make me feel so
small and fragile.

A lot of people in my life
probably don't realize how
scared I am to be anywhere near them.

That's because I
hide it with a mask.

I might be really
good at smiling
and keeping my
head up high, but
it takes nearly every ounce of
effort in my body to do so.

It takes 13 muscles to make
yourself smile.

For me, it feels
like it takes
hundreds.

But why am
I scared if
all it takes
is a smile?

I'd say I'm a pretty
nice person.

Now, I know for
a fact that some
people, specifically
the ones that this story is about,
will beg to differ, and that's
perfectly fine.

That's *your* opinion.

Anyways, I always
try to be as nice as I can to
everyone around me.

Whenever *they*
get near me, though?

Well, you don't
even *know*.

It feels like
this massive cloud of
negativity, hate, resentment,
anger, stress, pain, and any
other terrible thing
you can feel just
looms over me and won't leave until
they are *so* far away from me.

The worst part?

The cloud *lingers.*

It just sits over my head,
laughing at me like
I'm a circus freak.

It makes me
feel like I am one.

You know what else did that?

My.
Best.
Friend.

When I was trying
to end things with her, I had
to take a few days away from her
messages to think
things through correctly.

I didn't want to
make any hasty
decisions, you know?

During this time, she was
apologizing for something she
had said to me.

Something that had
triggered my absence
in the first place.

She called me several names,
one of which is below.

They hurt me more
than anything.

Terrible.

I won't lie, this
one was pretty deserved.

I had called her terrible
previously, which I shouldn't
have done and only
did because I was mad.

Why did I do it, though?

She texted my
(ex) boyfriend in the middle
of the night to criticize him.

I guess he wasn't
my boyfriend at the
time because we had just broken
up, but we were still on
good terms for the time-being.

I had forgiven him for having
broken up with me since he
apologized for it, so we stayed friends.

He had been interested
in getting back together
eventually, so I told him
that it was a "maybe."

My best friend knew
about this and
was apparently mad.

So how did *she*
plan on handling it?

Oh, I don't know….

"Would you be mad
if I messaged him?"

What.
Do.
You.
Think???

She's done this before, and
I've never liked it once.

What makes her think
I'd want her to now??

I told her not to message him, making
it very clear that I would be mad.

Her next message?
"I'm sorry."

Sorry??
Seriously????

Evidently, she obviously didn't
care what I thought.

Come to find out,
she had written him an
entire paragraph of nasty
comments to him informing
him that he is a terrible person
and should leave me alone.

I was *livid.*

That is a horrible
thing to do! I don't care who you
are, you don't criticize someone
so harshly like that!

Never!!

I let her know how angry I was.

I did tell her she was terrible.

I really did.

Do I regret it?

I actually don't.

It was true. Even though
I know I should feel bad for saying it,
I honestly don't.

And it feels good.

And I don't care.

You are terrible if you send a message to
someone talking about all of their flaws.

Eventually, we'll
get to the part where
my best friend did this to me, but
that is for future discussion.

For now, though,
I'm going to continue
with what I said to
her about the ordeal.

I told her that
she needed to butt-out
— that she didn't need
to be in every aspect of my life.

Afterall, I sure wasn't for her, but
I didn't expect to be.

Look, I was mostly
just mad about her
new friendship, okay??

But I wasn't wrong, either.

There was literally
zero need for her
to message him.

I never asked her to, and she never
even considered how I'd feel.

Sure, she'd asked, but she didn't
even care enough
to consider my answer.

That's what angered
me the most.
*Anger*ed?
I'm still mad.

The fact that she just went
ahead and texted him *despite* my
extreme disapproval.

Look, I know, I know, everyone
has the right to freedom of speech
and whatever else, but
if you're going to say
something *no matter
what,* just don't ask if
you can do it in the first place.

No, she didn't need
my approval, but
she shouldn't have
asked me if it didn't
matter in the first place.

That's senseless, and it
just causes trouble.

Like, see what happened??

She should've never
even asked.

To stray off topic
just a little bit here,
I want to recall something
that happened recently
before I forget it.

It happened today, actually, not
long before I am writing
this right now.

My school had a motivational
speaker stop by to talk to us
about mental health.

His name is Cory Greenwood,
and he has said some
of the most relatable
things I have heard in
a long while.

He spoke the truth.

One of the things he said stood
out to me the most.

He was talking about loss
and some things that people
might go through, such
as losing a pet or loved
one or-
losing a friend.

That hit home, but it
wasn't those words
that struck me.

It was these:
"Whether you lose a
loved one or have to
put down a pet, or
even when your best friend
stabs you in the back so deep you
don't think you'll ever get that
knife out again."

When I tell you
my heart stopped,
it felt like the *world* stopped.

Even the air around me
seemed to freeze.

Every molecule.

Every *sound.*

His voice felt far away,
distant as if he was yelling
to me from across a ravine.

My entire body, which
had included my
shaking leg, stopped.

In that moment, his
words hit their mark.

Bullseye.
My heart had
ached in that small
moment that it took
him to speak those
bloodied words.

Usually, speakers
like that don't make me tear
up, but he did.

Salty water had
flooded my eyes to the
brim, not quite spilling over
but not quite having enough
room for more, either.

Never has anything
struck me so hard, with so much
force and so much power, as
those words did in
that moment.

At the time,
I had actually
grabbed my chest,
right over my heart,
because I could physically feel
it cracking unevenly
down its center.

Broken pieces,
like shards of glass,
separated from itself, expelling
any tiny bit of
grief that I had
left then.

All that had
remained was anger,
hatred, and pure
disgust that someone
could ever be so cruel
to the person they
claimed to love so dearly.

Yet even though
my body was
flooded with tons
of emotions, the
only thoughts in my mind were,
"Does she feel guilty?"
"Does this strike
her just as hard
as it does me?"
"Does she even care?"

And that's the hard part
about all of this.

She acts like she doesn't care,
but I *know* she does.

You want to know
how I know?

Because *I know her.*

I tell myself most
of the time that
I had been under
the wrong impression
the whole time about
who she was, but in
reality, I wasn't at all.

I know her.

She was the girl who would
always apologize to me, even
if she did nothing wrong.

She was the girl who constantly
needed to know that I was okay
if I wasn't feeling too good.

She was the girl who, despite every
argument we had, always
came back to her best friend.

I know she cares because there
is no way that you don't.

There is *no way*
you can tear a
person's heart to
shreds and not feel
a single drop of
remorseful emotion.

I don't care how much
of a face she puts on, or how heavy
of a mask she wears,
I *know* she is sorry.

Somewhere, deep-down,
under that icy,
bitter-cold exterior, she cares.

She always has, and
you can't just turn that off.

I know this
because *I* have
always cared.

Despite how many
times I have come
home from school
wanting to leave
this place, feeling
like the ground
had been ripped out
from underneath my
feet, wanting to shy
myself away from
everyone for the rest
of my life, simply because
of *her*, I. *Still.* Care.

I *still* love her, and it
burns like *nothing* I have
ever felt before in my
entire life.

No matter how many times she
has cut a hole in me so
deep that I can't fill it.

No matter how many
times I have collapsed
on my bathroom floor,
exhausted from crying about what
she did to me.

No matter how many best friends I've
seen together, knowing they're
having fun and me
being jealous because I lost the
one relationship I had like that.

I still care.

And there is literally
nothing that will
make me stop.

I used to believe that if
someone ever hurt me that
badly, I would hate them.

I wasn't wrong,
because I do hate her.

I honestly don't
care if that sounds
terrible or if it makes
some people
uncomfortable to hear.

It's just the truth.

I have every right
to hate someone
for hurting me so badly,
just like I would
understand if someone
hated me, right?

Some of you are going to
disagree, and that's fine.

I get it.

"Hate is a strong word!"
"You should never
hate anyone!"
"Hate is the reason
why the world is
such a bad place!"

But it isn't technically hate
that makes everything
so bad in the world.

It's the people.

You can hate
someone and still be
polite to them.

Some people
may hate you and
you not even know it.

What do you think
mean girl behavior
in movies is based off of?

Hating each other
behind their backs.

I'm not saying it's okay.

I certainly don't
like hating people, but
sometimes someone does
enough to make you wish they
just lived somewhere
else entirely.

I hate that feeling.

I hate *hate*.

I hate having this
overwhelming feeling of loathing
towards a single human being that
I just can't shake, no matter how
hard I try to make those
feelings go away.

And what I said earlier
about hating *her?*

It *was* true. *Is* true.

But I also love her.

Way more than I'd
care to admit.

And yes, you can
love and hate someone.

It is that feeling
when you want something
so, *so* badly but you
know that you can
never have it.

When you want
to buy something but
you can't stand it because
it costs too much.

Too much money.

Or too much energy.

Or even too much heartbreak.

You shouldn't be forced to
put more effort into a
friendship than the other
person contributing.

Or, rather, the person
who is *supposed* to be contributing.

Not that she didn't contribute.

Of course she did.

I'm not at all saying that I was
a better friend than her.

Towards the end,
though, it felt like she just...
...gave up.

And, if I'm being honest,
I think I may have, too.

I was just done.

With everything.

I was done trying.

Fighting.

Fighting to be the friend she loved the
most like I always had been.

Fighting to hold
my ground in a losing
battle against two
people who were not on my side.

Fighting to keep myself from
losing my mind over the fact
that it felt like everything
I loved was slipping
from my fragile hands.

I was done.

You can take my white flag.

Take it.

Shred it up, burn it, stain it,
do *whatever* you want
with it because I'm so sick
and tired of being stepped
all over and treated like
the garbage that they
made me feel like.

I'm tired of holding onto my white
flag, waiting for something to change.

To *give*.

I thought something would
but now I realize that
that isn't going to happen.

Not in quick enough
time, anyways.

I would like to
believe that she'll
come around eventually, but
it certainly isn't happening
anytime soon.

I don't expect
her to, in all honesty.

I have fully
prepared myself to
be let down by
the simple fact
that she just was
never meant to be
in my life for the long run.

And that's okay.

I'm okay...
...right?

I think so…

To be honest, I haven't really
thought much about how I'm doing.

I mean, I considered
it, but I never actually went
into detail with myself about anything.

I guess I just…assumed
that everything was fine.

That I was happy.

Am happy.

Am I though?

I want to say yes,
but then again…

There have been
countless nights when
I have proven to myself that I am
really not doing so good.

So am I *actually*
as okay as I say I am?

I don't even know anymore.

One part of me
feels extremely happy
all of the time.

I love my friends,
my parents, and
my life.

But another part of
me feels completely
numb and empty.

There are times when
I'll catch my reflection
in a mirror as I
pass it by, and when
I see my face, all I can think about is
how unwanted I feel by the people
who are now in my life.

Not because
they're mean, or because
they aren't good people.

They are, and I
love them so much.

It's just...

My trust has been ripped apart, and I
don't think some Elmer's glue
or Scotch Tape is going to put
it back together again.

Maybe it can, I don't know.

It certainly doesn't
feel like it.

Nearly every time
I talk to someone new,
or even someone I'm close with at
times, I have this overwhelming
sense of worry and fear
that the things they're telling
me, no matter how nice
they are, aren't genuine.

I tend to feel like
people are lying to me,
or that they are trying
to trick me into thinking
they like me when they don't.

That's messed up, isn't it?

So messed up.

It really is.

It's ridiculous to feel this way,
and I know it all too well.

I know I can trust them,
and I know they wouldn't
lie to me like that, but the thoughts
just appear and they love to make
themselves at home without my approval.

Let me tell a short
story about what I mean.

It happened to me
very recently, actually.

You may laugh, and
that's okay.

I really noticed something wasn't right
when I started talking to this guy that I liked.

My friend had given
him my number at his request,
and he proceeded to message
me to begin getting to know
me a little better.

He knew I liked him,
and he liked me.

When he first said hi to me, I was
so very excited about it.

I never thought I
would be talking to him.

That pure excitement
didn't last for very
long, though.

I was soon
overcome with
this irrational fear
that I wasn't talking
to the person I
thought I was talking to.

I thought someone
was playing some kind of sick,
perverted joke on me.

Nobody was, thankfully, but
I was terrified at the time
that they were.

It took me an entire evening to
believe that it was him.

All because of a
broken string of trust
and misleading love.

Nobody should have
that kind of affect on anyone.

Absolutely not.

Nobody should be able
to make another person
fear trusting another
human being.

That is disgusting.

It makes me ill, and not just
because it happened to me.

It's because I know
that it has happened
to so many others.

People who don't deserve that
type of pain and heartbreak.

At this point, I've
written about so many
things, I can't even remember what
I haven't mentioned yet
because there is so much
that just needs to be included and *heard*.

I do want to talk
about one thing, though.

Our last good
moment.

You know, you may
have heard of things
like your last good year,
or your last good day.

I'm talking about a moment.

A single moment.

One moment that
I look back on now
and my heart swells
with pain because I know
that I will never get
it back again.

Ever.

It was our last sleepover.

We had such an
amazing time, but
somehow, deep-down,
I *knew*, my body *knew*, that every
glimpse around her house,
every time I sat on her bed,
every time I held her
puppy and pet her
cat, would be the last
time I would ever do those
things ever again.

The moment I
walked out her front
door, I knew I would never be
coming back through.

I didn't act like it.

How could I have?

But my heart beat
a little faster, my thoughts
raced, and my eyes desperately soaked
up every ounce of memory
they could of what everything
looked like before it
all came crashing down around me.

Around *us*.

Around everything
we built together.

Every picture I
drew for her, every
gift I bought for her,
everything glared at
me from her walls
and her little white shelves.

Everything stared at
me as I walked out that door
for the very last time.

And I *did* know it would
be the last time.

Once that door
shut behind me, and
I watched her wave
out the window,
hearing her dog
barking, it was 100x
more difficult to get in
my car to go home that day.

You may experience
a moment in your life
when it dawns on you that a
situation might just be hopeless.

It's that moment in
movies when the loved-by-all
hero desperately tries to
save the only person
who really means
anything to him, the only
person he truly wanted,
needed to save, but can't.

He can't because
they've fallen too far,
or they've already been
stolen away by the monstrous
villain, or even because fate can't
be altered by anyone.

Even heroes.

But the truth is, heroes simply
can't save *everyone*.

And sometimes, to
save the most things, you have to
sacrifice the one thing
you love the most.

See, the sacrifice that
I made? It was the hardest
possible thing that I could've
given up, and to be honest,
I have never been the same since.

Now, I'm not calling
myself a hero or anything,
because everyone has
to make sacrifices every
now and then.

But this one was big.

Let me tell you a little bit
more about myself.

I'm an extremely
shy person before
you get to know me.

It's very difficult for me to be
brave enough to go up and
talk to new people.

This means that when
I make (close) friends with
people, which isn't many, I
try my best to hold onto them.

With an iron grip.

Until the skin on my palms gets
ripped from my hands, I will
not let you go.

Not until I
absolutely have to.

Not until it is hurting you or I
worse by holding on
rather than letting go.

Not until we know it
isn't just some
ridiculous fight that
we'll get over within
a week.

I need to know that the pain either
of us have caused can no
longer be salvaged before
I decide to pull that
trigger and release
my grip on you
and everything we
have put so much
effort into together.

And *this* sacrifice was decided
under that knowledge.

No matter how sick
it makes me feel.

No matter how critically
severe the pain is.

It was the right thing to do.

For myself.

For…
…*her?*

I don't know that one.

I really hope it was
the best thing for her, though.

I'm sure it was.

It had to have been.

That game of
emotional tug-of-war
that we always played
couldn't have been
the better option for her.

It wouldn't be for anybody.

Shouldn't be.

Why would it?

Why would you
choose to continue
putting your own mood
at the mercy of how
another person is feeling?

Personally, I have no
idea why I did that.

Every time she would
be sad or feel down
or stressed in any way,
it would reflect in
the way I acted that day.

I was moody constantly
because, not only was
I dealing with my own emotions, but I
was dealing with hers, too —
this whole other
person who, might I add,
was emotional just like me.

I'm not blaming her.

It was no one else's decision
but my own to do that.

Also, I have to add that it
isn't a bad thing to be
an emotional person.

That isn't what I
meant by what I said before.

Being emotional doesn't
make you a burden
to the people around
you simply because
you are a bit more sensitive to
certain things and situations.

In my experience,
emotional people are
usually pretty good at reading
other people's emotions by
just looking at them.

That is a good thing.

If you can read
people's emotions
well, you are able to tell if you
hurt them in some way.

And I know
that she could read
my emotions perfectly.

She knew she was hurting me.

It was as clear as day.

Maybe not to
most people, but
to her, yeah.

She knew me better
than anyone, and she
knew how to cut
straight to the bone.

That's exactly what
she did.

She sawed and
sawed at the marrow
and the tissue, tearing away at
the only support system
I had until I was left
with a pile of an unorganized
mess of myself.

Was it intentional?

It feels like it.

She says that she,
they, didn't do anything
to hurt me...
...but what if they did?

I'm genuinely asking.

I don't mean for that to sound
like one of Taylor Swift's
(amazing) songs.

It just happens to.

But, to be honest,
the woman *does*
make a good point.

People tell you that
they never *meant* to hurt you.

"Nobody ever does."

It's what everyone says when they are
guilty of wrongdoing.

It's what everyone says to try
and make themselves feel better
about what they've done.

There's no need
to lie to yourself, though.

You might not have specifically
had it in mind to
hurt me, but the fact that you
did it in the first place
means that you never cared
enough to prevent it from
happening at all.

And that hurts.

People should never
allow their friends to
get hurt if it's in their
power to stop it.

I didn't think
that had to be explained,
yet here we are.

You wanna know what sucks?

Conflicting thoughts.

Like the ones telling me that I should block her.

Telling me that I should find her contact and simply delete it from my phone entirely.

But will I ever do that?

No.

I can't.

I *physically* can't.

Just *no*.

Why?

Because every
time I somehow
find the nerve to do it,
I can't help but think this one
single thing:
"What if she needs me?"

That's what I'm
worried about.

I'm worried about
someone who doesn't
want me to end up needing me.

I have no clue how that makes
sense so don't ask me.

It just scares
me to death.

What scares me, exactly, is that there
may be some off-chance
(in my head, anyways)
that if I blocked her, she might
end up hurt or in trouble some day
and if she were to message me
or call me for help then I
wouldn't be able to be there
and I would never know.

That's a lot, I know,
and it's probably confusing.

In all honesty, though, if she
were to message me right
now because she was
in danger for some reason,
I would help her as best
as I could in a heartbeat.

But if I blocked her, I wouldn't be
able to be there for her.

That would kill me.

It kills me even
knowing that my
brain works this way,
thriving on this one shred of hope
that she might just reach
out to me for something
other than forgiveness
that she'll simply never get.

I don't think she
knows that, though.

She reached out to
me just the other
day, actually.

Told me she was sorry.

That she misses me.

Don't do that.

I hate that.

Don't you dare come to me to
tell me that you miss
hanging out and
that you miss coming
to my house and
going to the pool.

I don't want to
hear it, because for
the past few months,
that is *all* I've missed.

Or, rather, only a small
portion of what I've missed with you.

You're sorry about the way things
ended between us?

I'm sorry that
I gave you so many chances
to prove me wrong.

I gave you so many
opportunities to change what you
were doing before the
inevitable happened.

I gave you your choices.

And I knew mine.

Yeah, I know I said before
that I would've felt guilty
asking her to drop
her friendship with
that girl, but now that
I think about it, I really
don't think I would
feel guilty at all.

It sounds horrible,
I know, but it's
the truth.

Letting myself feel
any sort of remorse
for those two after what they did
would be a crime to myself.

Not that I deserve
some kind of justice
or anything.

That's not what I'm saying.

But that friendship,
from what I'm guessing,
is not going to get very far.

And if it does, then
good for them.

I mean that in the snarkiest
way possible, too.

Surprised?

Let's be honest,
did anybody reading
this actually expect
me to be happy for them
for building a lasting friendship??

Did you expect me
to welcome their
bond with open arms?

Seriously??

Absolutely not.

Not a single
chance.

What?

Not every thought that I have about
them is going to be nice or
positive or optimistic about
them in some way.

I have bad thoughts, too.

It's normal when you've
been hurt by them.

If you've never
been betrayed by
someone you thought would
never leave you, then
you have no idea.

You'd be shocked
by how many bad
thoughts you can have.

Am I going
to go into detail about some
different ones that
I've had about the two of them?

No.

I will never do that.

I have at least
that much decency.

I'll just say
that they haven't
always been the
nicest things to
think about someone.

I'm not proud of it,
but I honestly don't
really care, either.

What?

It's not like I'm ever going
to say them out loud to anyone,
so why does it
matter so much?

I know that they've
had their fair share
of bad thoughts about me, so.

I mean, I won't lie, it does
hurt to think that my
used-to-be best friend would
think bad things about
me, but it also hurts me
that *I* am capable of
thinking bad about *her*.

Don't ask me
how that works.

I used to not
be able to think
bad things about
her, like when we
first stopped being friends
with each other.

I have no idea
what happened, though.

I'm not sure you can call it
maturing, but I know that it was some
sort of growth for myself
that allowed me to be
able to think like that.

Before, I couldn't
think a single bad
thought about her.

But now…?

What I wouldn't do to be able
to remember her
in a positive manner.

But I can't.

Every time I see
her face, every time
I hear her voice, I can't see *or* hear
anything other than the girl
that stabbed me in
the back with the dull
blade that she was
wielding in her hidden fists.

Each glance at her
brings back the pain
that I felt from her
torturous departure.

Like picking at a scab.

Hmm, I feel like I've mentioned some
things in this story that I said
I was going to talk about and
then never actually talked about (oops).

There's a few things, so here's
a list to remind myself (and
you, I suppose):

1. Homecoming
2. Balloons
3.

...okay, maybe the list
isn't as long as I thought it would
be, so I guess that's nice.

Anyways, we'll
talk about homecoming
now, I suppose.

This was probably
one of the biggest
breaking points for our
friendship.

It wrecked us and pretty
much any faith we had
in the other.

As I said before,
it was homecoming,
and everybody was
stressed and freaking out.

Actually, to be clear,
it was about a month
before homecoming.

But the stress still factors in.

I'll tell you exactly why.

My best friend and I had made
plans to go with each other to the
homecoming dance
at our school.

We made these
plans approximately
one or two months
before the dance,
or maybe it was even
before that previous summer
had started.

I'm not entirely sure
when the plans were made, but
they had been made, and she
even wanted me to promise
that we would go together,
even if one of us (or both)
was dating someone at the time.

I hadn't intended on lying to her.

Okay, that sounds *really* bad.

Let me specify.

I wasn't lying to
her when I had made
that promise.

We were best friends
then. Of course I'd
love to have gone with her no
matter what my situation
was at the time of the dance.

But I didn't, and here's why.

In this month or so before the
dance, her and I had gotten into
an argument and neither
of us were doing anything
to let us make up.

I can't remember
exactly what the fight
was about, but I'm
pretty sure it may have
been about me sitting
somewhere else at lunch.

Either way, the fight
had caused us to stop
talking for a couple of
weeks, and I wasn't
sure if we were ever
going to make up again.

At least, not before homecoming.

So, I did the only
thing I could think of.

I asked the guy I was seeing if he'd
go with me instead.

Big mistake.

I kid you not,
a day had went by
after I'd asked him
when my best friend reached
out and apologized to me.

A. Single. Day.

What are the chances??

That is literally the perfect
example of the kind of luck
that I have about
roughly 94.7% of the time.

Now, I was stuck.

Between a rock and
a very, very hard place.

What in the world
was I supposed to do??

I am genuinely
asking because
I had literally zero clue.

I *still* don't fully
know what would've
been the right thing to do.

I clearly chose
the wrong one, though.

Again with the
bad luck?? Jeez, universe,
can't you ever
give a girl a break???

I'm trying my
best, here.

My best was
never good enough.

It never felt like it, anyways.

That's not the
point, though.

Here's what happened.

She texted me and
told me that she
was sorry about the
fighting, and she
wanted everything to be
okay between us again.

I agreed because I
missed her so much.

But I hadn't told her yet.

It took a few days before I
actually told her
that the homecoming
plans had changed.

It took her asking
for me to say it.

Before, I just
hadn't had the heart,
and I could never
work up the nerve to tell her.

But now, with her
questioning me
about it, I had no
choice but to be
brutally honest with her.

So I told her, and
she didn't take it well.

Not that I had expected her to.

I knew she'd be mad.

Heck, *I* was mad.

Mad at myself.

Mad at the fact that I had
changed up my mind like that
when she had made me promise her that
we would go together.

I *never* break my
promises if I can help it.

But in all honesty,
I blame it on her.

You can disagree.

She picked the
fight before homecoming.

She was constantly
mad at me for
wanting to hang out
with the guy I was seeing.

I always heard from
her that I was
choosing him over
her all the time,
which definitely was
not true in the slightest!

She told me that
I *always* had to
pick *her* before I
ever picked *him.*

What the heck???

That is actually
the most selfish thing
I have ever heard in my life.

It's crazy to think that she
actually said that,
but she did.

I was in disbelief.

I get it in a
sense that you
really want to hang
out with your best friend,
but you simply cannot
have all of my time.

I had to split it.

It was only fair
to him that I did.

Splitting my time,
though, was apparently
not ever going to be
good enough for her.

Anyways, skip
ahead to about a
few nights before homecoming.

Her and I make
one decision that we thought,
or I thought, would fix
everything about
the whole situation.

Okay, maybe not *everything*, but
most things, at least.

I'd stay with him
for the first half, and then
go with her for the second.

It seems fool-proof,
doesn't it?

Well, it wasn't.

I thought so, too,
until the night of the dance.

You see, after I had spent
the first hour and a half with
my date, I made the
attempt to make the switch
to my best friend.

However, there
was one problem.

She wasn't making the switch.

She told me to
just forget it.

I asked why.

She refused to give
me a legitimate reason.

She told me to just stay
with him and that she was
perfectly okay with it.

I knew for certain
that she was not okay with it.

There was something
very wrong, but she
literally would not
tell me and a dance is
not necessarily the best
place to discuss something like that.

She kept walking
away from me.

I ended up just
staying with him because
she wouldn't tell me why she
had changed her mind all
of the sudden.

I checked her location after about
20 minutes and was
shocked to see that she had gone home.

Was I mad?

Yeah.

Outraged.

Not at that, but the fact that she
had made such a big
deal about splitting my
time in the first place
just for her to leave.

I didn't really care
at the time because
I was mostly just
worried about her.

I mean, I did care,
but I wasn't going to bring
it up right then in the moment.

There were bigger things
to worry about.

Like what was going on with her?

I was so scared.

I thought something
bad had happened.

She didn't tell me
until after the dance.

Apparently, the
reason why she went
home early was because
she was feeling left out that night and
felt like no one wanted her around.

She explained to me
that she saw me having fun and
didn't want to bother me.

It wouldn't have
bothered me, though.

I was looking forward
to spending time
with her at the dance.

If she wouldn't have left, we
would've had fun. I know it.

But she did.

I hate this part
of our story,
because it's the
very moment I knew
that we were
officially falling apart.

I mean, it was
kind of obvious
before, but this was
the moment when I
actually knew that
we were beyond the
point of being able
to save ourselves.

To save us.

To save what we had.

And it hurts, ya know?

It's that silent realization when it
finally dawns on
you that you are losing one of
the things that you adore
most in this world.

And there is
nothing that you
can do now to stop her
from fading away.

There was nothing
I could've said,
done, or suggested
that would've been
a helpful idea.

The only thing
was for me to walk out.

So that's what I did.

I wish I could say
that our story didn't have to
end like this.

I wish I could say
that I'm not clumsy
when it comes to certain things.

Like holding on.

I've had it happen too many
times where I've let balloons
go at parties.

They fly away
and drift into the
sunlight, their departure
blinding you when you
watch them leave.

Your hand now feeling empty.

I would like to mention a few
more things before I wrap this up.

One of them is
that she was never
there for any of
my birthdays.

I had three in total
while we were friends.

One of them she couldn't go to my
party because she had
a basketball tournament
that day for our school.

The other two?

We just so happened
to be fighting during
those ones.

Coincidence??

I don't know.

You tell me.

Why the heck was I there for
every birthday of hers,
but she was never there
for *any* of mine???

I'm not really mad about that, and
I never really was, but
I find it very strange
and a little upsetting.

Also, every fight that was happening
during my birthday was always
fixed or apologized for
by her not long after my
birthday had passed.

So, would I go back and do it all again
if I had the chance?

Yeah.

Yeah, I would.

I don't know why.

...

No, I do.

I do know why.

She taught me a lot about myself.

She taught me a lot about
her that I was missing.

She taught me
a lot about the kinds
of people that you
can find in this bitter world.

There are two kinds.

The kind who
will be there for you,
and the kind who won't.

There is no in-between.

It's all
or nothing.

You can't just
be there for part
of the time and back
out when things
get remotely difficult.

What happened
to having my back?

What happened
to wanting to be there for
me when the things
in my life got too difficult for me
to handle by myself?

That all went down the
gutter, didn't it now?

But it's fine.

It's cool.

I'm over this little petty
back and forth thing that
we got going on.

I'm through.

Here's the thing.

She acts like she's happy now,
but the truth is, there is no way
you can be that happy.

Not after something
like that, I mean.

I know I wasn't fully okay at first.

I'm still not.

I still hold that heavy chip on my
shoulder that will never fade.

She must, too...
...right?

Right?

I just have one
final question for her.

*Do you remember
saying this to me?*

"I'm obviously not
going to go be best friends
with her. If you're this
paranoid and you don't
trust that I won't then
why are we even friends?"

I'm being paranoid??

I'm the one who
is overthinking
your guys' relationship???

Is it being paranoid
if I'm right...?

You can never fully know
who is going to hurt you.

There is no way to
see into the future.

You just have to look out for yourself, because it
will always happen when you least expect it.

When you think you've found someone to trust.

Be careful, though.

Afterall, the devil used to be an angel.

Best friends forever?

Yeah.

Forget it.

*"I was 18 when I wrote that.
That's the age you are when you think someone
can actually take your [boyfriend]. Then you grow up
and realize no one takes someone from you
if they don't want to leave."
- Taylor Swift*

Author's Note

I need to get this out there before I completely wrap this book up, so don't shut it and put it away on the shelf just yet, please.

A lot of people, after me having published this book, will probably think that me being a published author now will make me happy — that it will ease the pain of what happened. It doesn't. It really, *really* doesn't. Do you want to know the truth? Every time I see this book, I will think of her. Every time someone mentions anything about me having written this book, I will remember her and what she did to me. It might seem amazing to have a book published (which it totally is, don't get me wrong), but this book in particular was not worth the heartbreak that it took to get the story in the first place.

I thought writing this story, getting the truth out there, would help fix things. Most things, anyways. I thought it would take away all of the thoughts that continue to haunt me by writing them down for people to read, but it didn't. They're still here. I've tried so many things in an attempt to get over what happened and

nothing works. This book, while feeling like a form of therapy for me, did not heal me. It helped, sure, but I am definitely a long way down the road from being healed. I've come to accept the fact that it will take a long time for me to stop feeling so much sorrow from this. That's okay. Some people are just...they mean too much for you to be able to move on like that.
I know for a fact that I have healed significantly within the past few months. I'm not done healing, I know, but I'm doing better. The way I know is because...well, essentially, publishing this book was like locking it in that I really don't want to be friends with her anymore. Let's be honest, if someone wrote a book about you where all they do is vent about what you did, would you want them back??

Probably not.

I see now that the only reason she was able to hurt me so much was because I let her get close. When you let people get close, you expose your deepest fears to them. Sometimes, when you do this, they will turn around and use those fears against you. Like if they know you're scared of being alone, they threaten to leave you. Or if they know you're scared of people thinking you're not good enough, they'll talk down to you in abominable ways. This is called manipulation for those of you that don't know.

I'm not saying *at all* that it is bad to let people into your life. It just might take a few chances. Or a lot. But that's okay. I know it's hard, I know it hurts, but once you start to know what certain kinds of people look like, it gets easier. After her, I took some time for myself. I found my group of people that I love and cherish, and they appreciate me for me. I don't feel scared or anxious around them. Around them, I feel loved. I feel safe. I feel *wanted.* Those are my people. Those are the relationships that blossomed from my pain.

Even though I miss our friendship so much, I've accepted that I will never be close with her again.

That's final.

It hurts. But yeah. It'll be okay. I'll be okay. And the saddest truth is that despite how hard I've worked to publish this book, I would trade this and our entire story for a redo of our friendship. With the *old* her, not this new person that she has become.

Acknowledgements

Frankly, I can't believe I made it this far. It sucks that I had to go through so much heartbreak to produce this book, because it definitely wasn't worth it. It will never be worth it. But it did teach me so many things, and I wouldn't have made it this far if I didn't have the support of so many lovely individuals in my life.

Thank you to my incredible parents, Teresa and William Hurley, who have always, *always* been there for me. You have never given up on me throughout this entire journey, and you've always believed in me. I always knew that I could count on you. Writing this book was a roller coaster of emotions that I knew I could get through with you guys at my side for the whole ride. I love you guys so much.

Thank you to Austin Lucas, who has shown me so much support for as long as you've known me. You are such an amazing person that I am so lucky to have in my life. You're my ride-or-die, and I appreciate all the help you've provided me with for my book. The journey, specifically, is what I'm talking about. You never gave up believing in me. You were always wanting to know how my book was coming along, and the interest that you showed meant more to me than you could ever imagine. You told me you were proud of me when I told you I was almost done with my book, and I thought it was the sweetest thing. I love you, All-Star.

Thank you to Cynthia Flener, who has been the most supportive friend I could ask for. She was with me through everything that happened, giving me advice when I needed it and letting me vent to her when I had to get stuff off of my chest. I have to credit the girl who kept me sane when I felt like I was losing my mind through all of this — the girl who never let me give up on myself. I love you, girl.

Thank you to my younger self. :) I gotta give her some credit. She never stopped believing in herself, even when she felt like she would never get published. If she could see us now, she would be brimming with joy with that crooked little smile of hers.

Thank you to my beta readers, Paisley Fellers, Emmalyn Splitter, and Malina Luckhart. I appreciate all the feedback that you guys gave. You all helped me finalize my book, and you checked for grammatical errors for me in case I missed anything. I loved your honesty with my writing, and the little compliments that you'd give every now and then really helped my confidence in my writing grow. Even though it was a sudden request, you guys sprang on the opportunity to help me out and it means the world to me. I love you guys. You will always have a special place in my heart.

Thank you to my rocks, Jennifer Keith and E. G. Keith. You guys are the entire reason I am a published author. You helped me through the entire process, and it literally means so much to me. I couldn't have ever done it without you amazing people. (Also, for anyone reading this, go check out their books! They're awesome.)

Thank you to Tonya Wells, my lovely aunt, who not only tried to help me throughout this process, but she also took my beautiful "About the Author" photo for this book. Her business is Tonya Wells Portraits at Poetic Grace & Co. Portrait Studio located in downtown Fairbury, Illinois. She and her husband built their studio from the ground up, and their business blossomed from a decaying brick building to a gorgeous photography studio. The photos that she takes are absolutely breathtaking and she will forever be my first choice in photographers.

Last, but *certainly* not least, I would like to thank the person that this book is about. You know who you are, so I'm not saying a name. Why am I thanking you, exactly? Well, you gave me a story. You gave me this entire book. I just had to write it, design a cover for it, and slap my name on it. That's all. So, thanks. Thanks for the story, because I wouldn't have it without you. :)

About the Author

Miley Rae Hurley is a new author who, as of 2024, has just published her first book. She has been working hard for several years to fight through procrastination, self-doubt, and writer's block to finally reach her huge dream of being an officially published author. While she favors horror and romance genres, she decided to write about a recent heartbreak of hers to hopefully get it out there to readers that they are not alone in what they are going through. Writing has always been one of her favorite pastimes. She adores expressing herself through the use of similes, metaphors, and detailed descriptions of emotions. She wants her readers to feel her pain through her words. She wants her words to bleed every drop of passion that she pours into her writing. Whenever she gets the chance, she is reading new books to expand her extensive vocabulary, and when she's not reading, she's either creating art or making new memories with her friends that she adores so dearly. She is incredibly grateful for everything she has worked so hard for.

Stay tuned for more works by her if you enjoyed what you read.

And now…

Here is a little message that I *would* send to my old best friend if I were to say anything at all.

But I won't. So it ended up here…

hey. i don't know if u want to hear from me right now, or, frankly, if u ever want to hear from me ever again. these words are the last ones that i will ever say to u, hopefully, because it hurts too much to do so. i don't quite understand why we treated each other the way we did, because i knew our friendship would've been a great one if we had just knew better. u loved me, and i loved u. we had such a perfect friendship, but we let so much get in between us. we were obviously too immature to realize what we had before it was gone. i know now, but do u? do u even think about our friendship anymore? u probably don't, which i'd understand. i've tried to push it out of my mind, too. "tried." i can't, though. i have a few questions for u if u don't mind. i don't really know if i want answers to them, or what i'm looking for exactly, but i have to get them off of my chest. why did u do it? why'd u have to hurt me? why did u pick her over me??

was i not good enough? did i not make u happy? i don't understand why u couldn't just have my back for once. u told me i'd always be ur best friend. u told me i was the greatest friend anyone could have. u told me we'd go to college together and now i'm forced to look for colleges by myself. why did u lie? i know ur not perfect. i know i'm not perfect. but i loved ur imperfections. they made u who u are. did i have too many for u to love? was i just too much for u? i wasn't before. u were always there for me through every rocky journey, so what changed?? i can't even blame ur new friend because i realize now that there was no way she could've truly taken u from me if u weren't reluctant. u allowed it to happen, and why? i warned u so many times of the kind of person she is, and u never listened to me. even if she changed, even if i was somehow wrong, it didn't even cross ur mind to consider my opinion of her. best friends are supposed to pick each other first. u said that. u were the one who told me that. were u trying to get back at me because u thought i was picking my ex over u?? is that what this was??? i would never pick him over u. u should know that. the reason i picked him was because it would've never been fair for him if i were to pick u all of the time. i know that sounds bad, but put urself in his shoes for a second. how would u feel if the girl u loved kept picking someone else over u?? every time? i didn't do it every time. i did it whenever i was scared of losing him. do u even realize how difficult it was for me to have to choose between u guys so much?? do u know how many messages i received from the both of u complaining about how i don't pick either of u enough?? i'm only one person!! i can't be everywhere and with everyone at once!! i was so stressed about trying to hold onto the both of u and nobody knew!!! i never told either of u about it because there was nothing that could be done to fix it. what could u have done?? nothing. u probably would've told me that ur a burden to me and that i'd be better off without u. that isn't true. neither of u were a burden. but it was tearing me apart to have to decide so much. so yeah, maybe i thought that it'd be easier if i lost one of u. did i want to? no. but i was so sick of fighting to keep up with two demanding needs that were sucking all of the energy out of me. i would've never said this to ur face because i hate even writing it out, but i can't keep it in anymore. i'm sick of keeping certain feelings to myself simply because i don't want to upset u. this will not be a graceful goodbye. i never got a real goodbye, and i never gave one either. after u finish reading this, if u even read this at all, i never wish to speak to u ever again. i realize that we have to finish high school together, and graduate together, but after that, i hope i never have to see ur face or hear ur name mentioned in conversation. i hope i never have to listen to ur voice when u speak, and i hope to God that i never have to listen to ur laugh that i used to love so much. i want u gone from my memory, but i will never forget u. i will never forget what u did. i will never forgive u for what happened. i know i should. i know it's the right thing to do. i know people can't be at peace with themselves when they hold grudges. but i'm holding on tight. i don't think forgiving u will ever put me at peace after this. i am changed. i'm not going to be fixed by telling u that "oh, it's okay" or "everything's forgiven" or "it's all good" because it's not. it never will be. i can't just forget that. i tried so hard not to give up on us. i had so much faith in us that we would pull ourselves out of that crater that we called a friendship, but we never did and it ruined me. i sincerely hope that u treat her better than u treated me. i know that i'll treat my friends better. i made mistakes. plenty of them. trust me, that occurred to me several months ago. i really hope u realize what u did wrong. i've put a lot of thought into the things i did, and i will never not feel guilty. i'm sorry for all of the times that i hurt u. i'm sorry for every time i took my emotions out on u because i had no one else to go to. i'm sorry for every time u thought i was picking someone else over u. i was trying to be fair and i was clearly just hurting u in the process, which was so wrong. i'm sorry for every fight we had. i'm sorry for all of the times when my pride took over and i didn't want to apologize. i'm sorry for every time u thought u weren't a good enough friend for me. u were. u were the exact type of friend that i was hoping to find. i don't know why things had to end the way that they did, but i guess that's just how it was meant to happen. i tried so hard to be enough for u in the last few months that we were friends. i give up trying. this is goodbye. my final true words to u. i don't regret knowing u. i don't regret our friendship. i regret losing u. i loved u with my entire heart. every last ounce. i still do. why? why do i do this to myself??? i am never going to welcome u back into my life so why do i still love u?

there's another thing i want u to know. i want u to realize the kind of permanent damage that u have inflicted on me. think of a time when u found something really special. something that is really important to u. now, just imagine urself enjoying it so much, and then that joy becomes unimaginable fear that whatever it is that u hold close to u is just going to vanish. with everything that i come to love, i just feel absolute fear that any happiness i feel with that person is either not deserved or won't last long. now, it's hard for me to believe any promises made to me that they won't leave me or abandon me or stop loving me. u did that. U. the one person i thought i could trust with anything in the world. u broke every ounce of trust that i had in love. every single time someone tells me, "u don't have to worry, i won't leave u," i can't help but think to myself, "yeah, as if i haven't heard that before." my worry was right. i should've listened to my intuition when it told me who u were the first time.

i hate it. i hate that i was right. i hate our story.

i hate it so much. the memories, the laughs, the inside jokes, the secrets that we don't tell anyone else about ourselves because they're way too embarrassing. every place we used to go that i can't stand to be around because it just reminds me of us. every text message that i can't help but reread because i miss looking forward to hearing from u every day. every stuffed animal in my room that u gave to me that i can't decide whether i want to keep or tear to shreds. every song we used to listen to that plays in the car or in my earbuds, hurting my head trying to decide if i should turn it off or relish in how many memories it brings back. i hate them.

i hate all of it.

i hate that i love u.

300

www.ingramcontent.com/pod-product-compliance
Lightning Source LLC
Chambersburg PA
CBHW050954050426
42337CB00051B/835